ROW YOUR BOAT

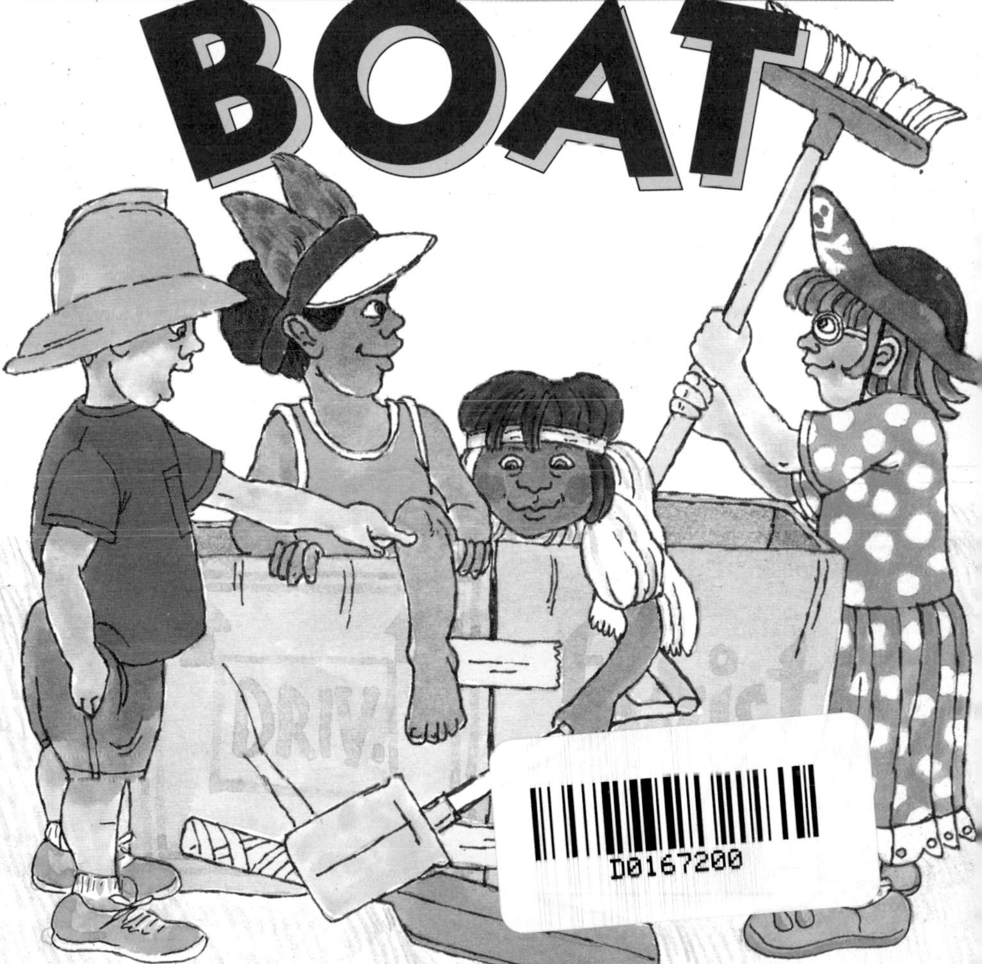

For Lizzie

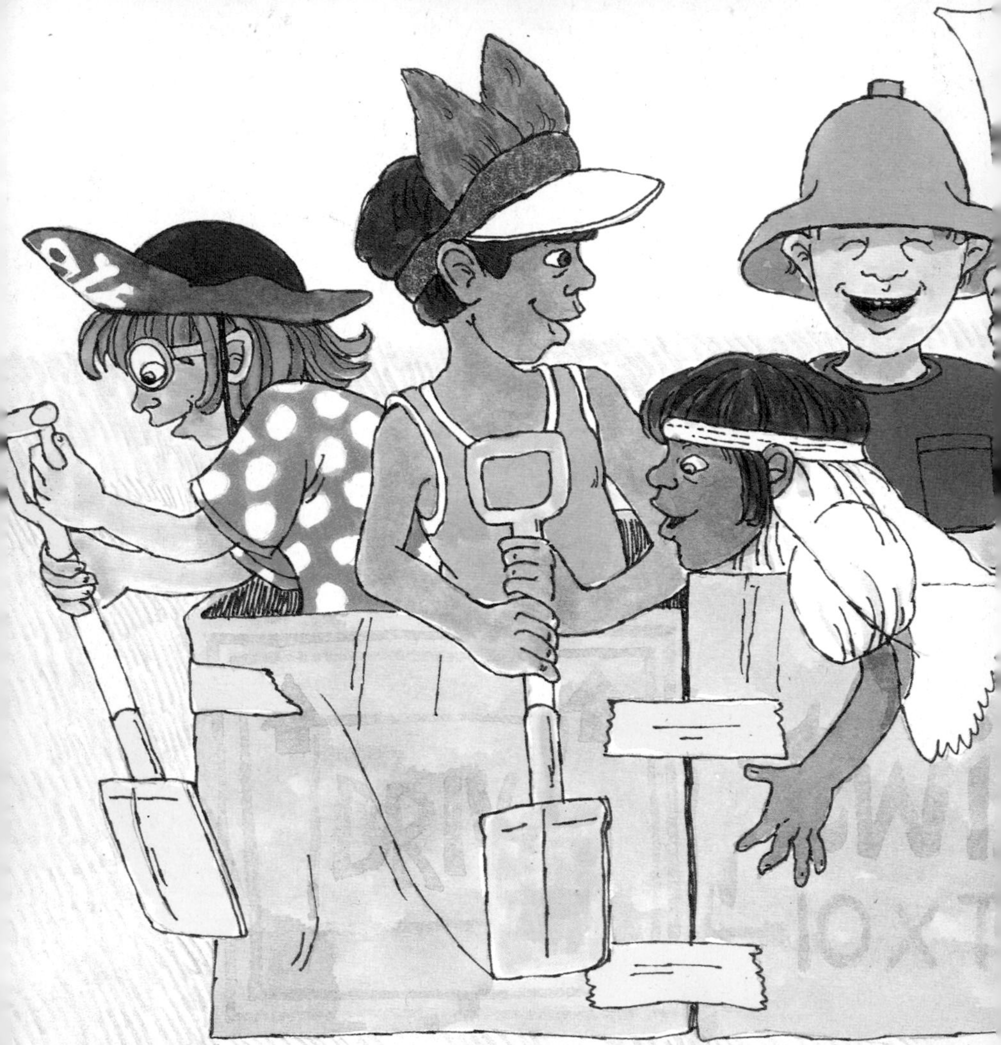

Row, row, row your boat,

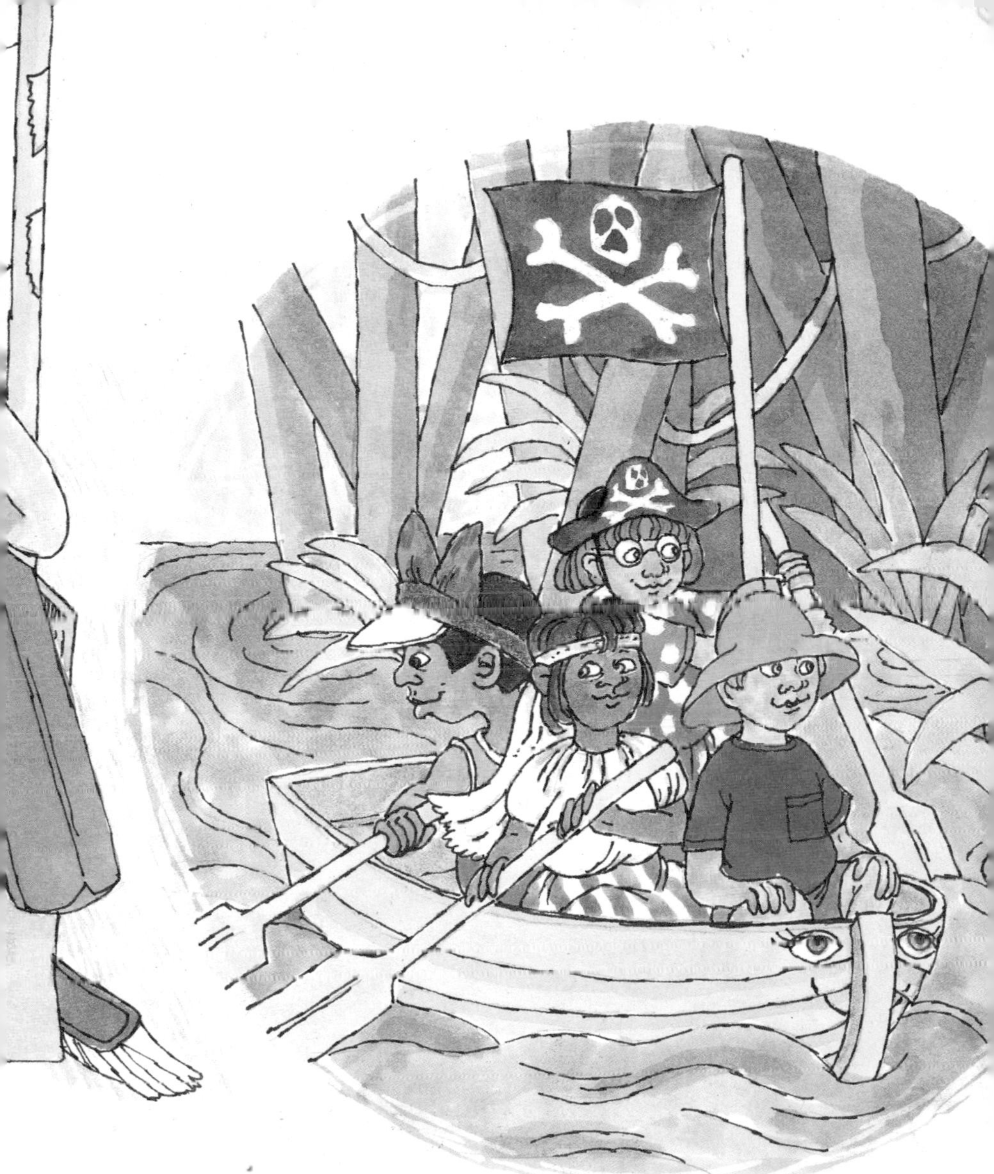

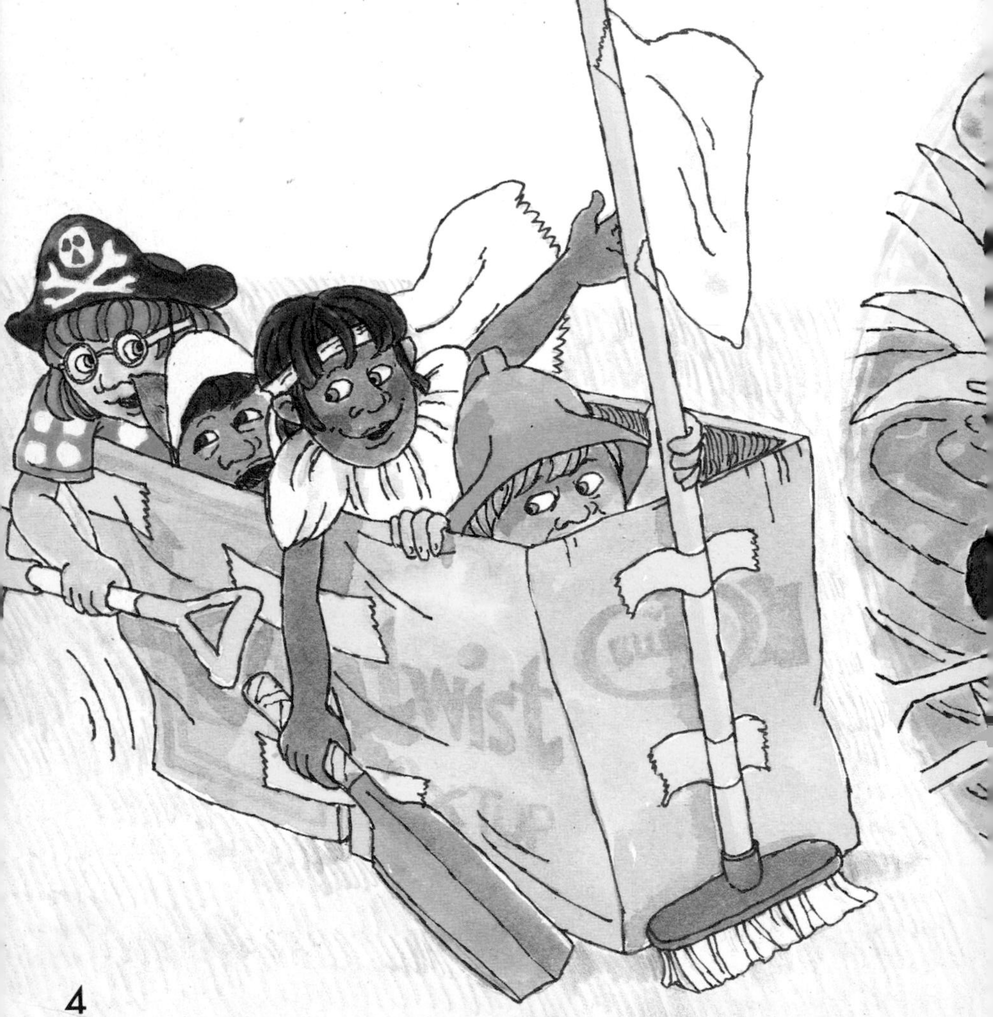

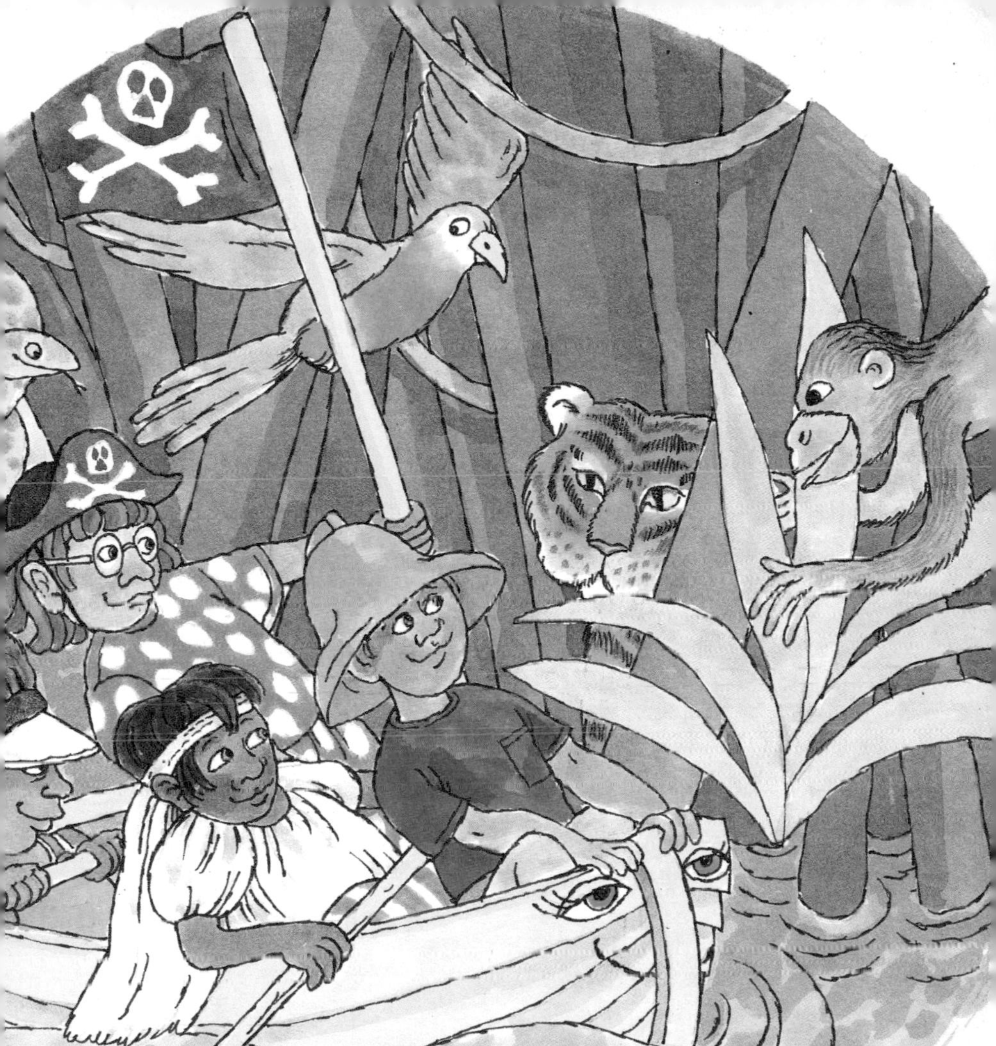

gently down the stream.

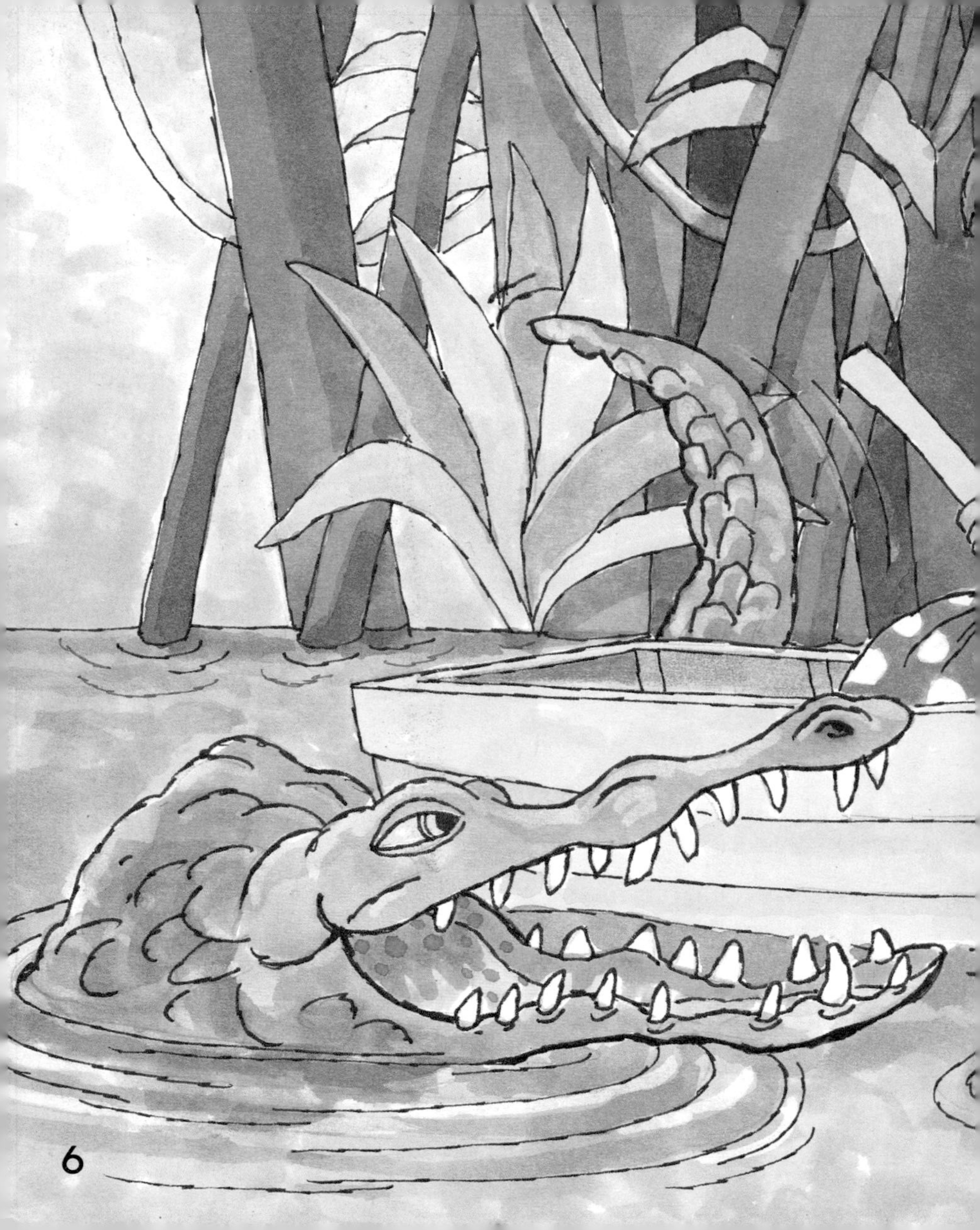

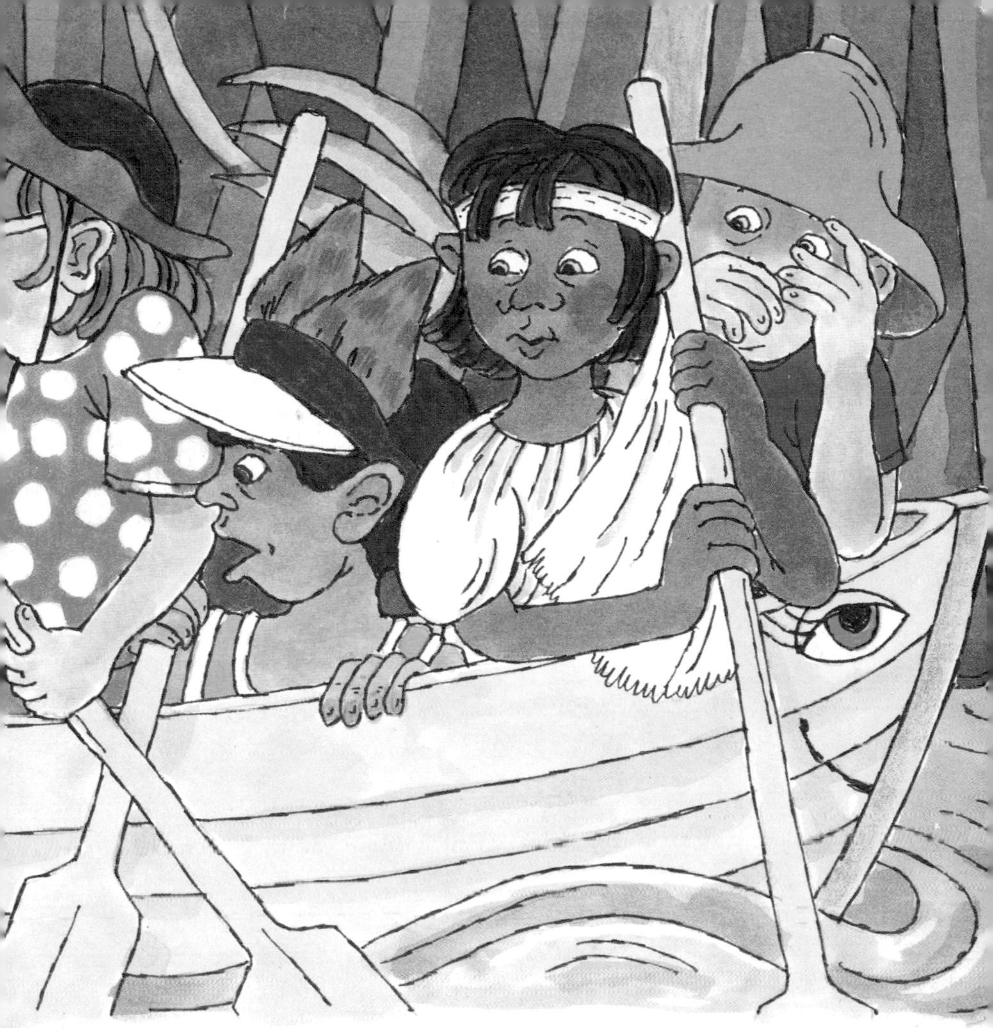

If you see an alligator...

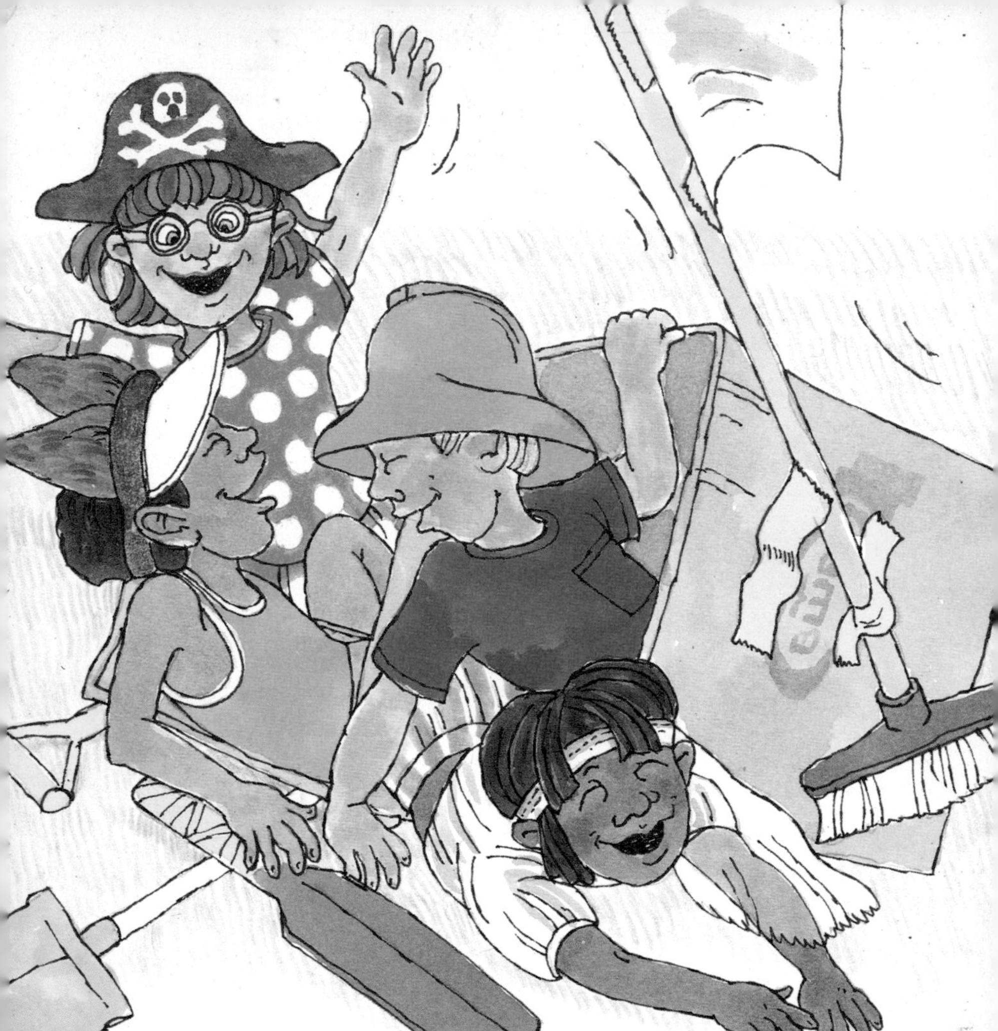

don't forget to SCREAM!